To Julia Crist,
Remember the Bay!
1996
Corinne M. Litzenberg

– *Flock Tales from the Flats* –

**The
Adventures of
Hanna Flats,
Captain Can
and their
Feathered Friends
from the Flats**

BY CORINNE M. LITZENBERG
ILLUSTRATED BY DAVID L. STEHMAN

First published in 1995 by
Decoy Magazine
P.O. Box 277
Burtonsville, Maryland 20866

ISBN 0-9631815-4-8

AUTHOR
Corinne M. Litzenberg

PROJECT EDITOR
Joe Engers

GRAPHIC DESIGNER
Karen O'Keefe

Library of Congress Catalog Card Number 95-70929

Printed in the United States of America

This book is dedicated to
Jack, Todd, Natalie and Sable, our black lab
and was inspired
by
Great Uncle Bob Litzenberg
(Renowned Flats Decoy Carver)

The SUSQUEHANNA FLATS

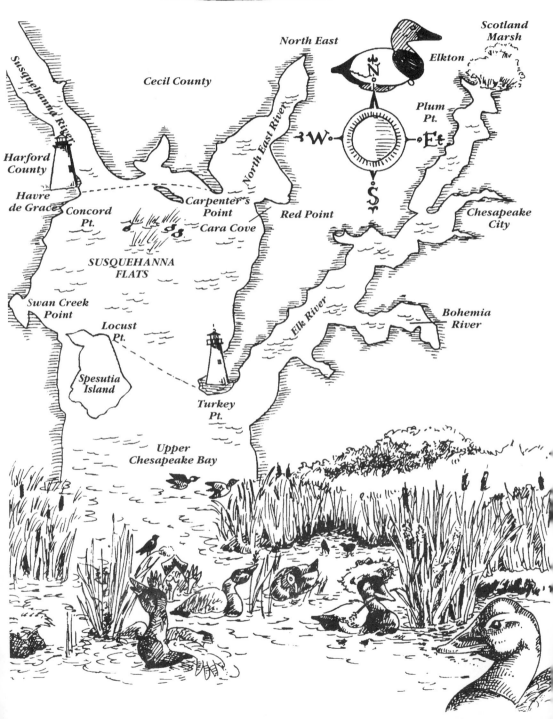

North East

Cecil County

Scotland Marsh

Elkton

Plum Pt.

N

W · E

S

Susquehanna River

Harford County

Havre de Grace

Concord Pt.

Carpenter's Point

Cara Cove

Red Point

Chesapeake City

North East River

SUSQUEHANNA FLATS

Swan Creek Point

Locust Pt.

Elk River

Bohemia River

Spesutia Island

Turkey Pt.

Upper Chesapeake Bay

"Close Duck Calls" was written for all children, especially those of the Upper Chesapeake Bay area. For many of us, we learned about the Flats in one of two ways. Some of us were self-taught because of a related interest, such as decoy collecting. Others learned the history from gunning stories passed down from generation to generation told by the ol' timers who still remember what hunting was like on the Flats in the 1930s. It is the author's hope that this historical, fictional account will enable children to appreciate and respect what we have (left) now and instill in them a stronger desire to preserve the Upper Bay and its surrounding waterways.

ne brisk, windy fall morning, at the crack of daybreak, the rising sun's lateral rays reflected upon a flock of canvasbacks feeding on wild celery and eel grass near Carpenter's Point. The entire rick of cans paddled through the thick harvest eating to their bills' content as they rode the rippling waves of the Flats. This particular flock swam on the outer edge of the imaginary line which stretched from Concord Point, near Havre de Grace, to Carpenter's Point. The southern imaginary line extended from Locust Point to Turkey Point. These make-believe lines mark the legal limits of the area known as the Susquehanna Flats. These shallow and hearty waters were a paradise for hunters and waterfowl in the 1930s. Along with the celery grazing canvasbacks, there were ricks of blackheads, redheads and a few

blackducks and pintails who frequented the fresh-water above the Chesapeake Bay. Old time hunters say, "When they took off in flight the skies were black with ducks!"

Among the congregations at this fowl feeding frenzy were the family of the regal Captain Can and Hanna Flats. A drake canvasback, Captain Can was a well respected and athletic bird from the Scotland Marsh. He was well known for his ability to dodge gunners' shots in a lightning bolt. His stubby wings, big body, long neck and wedged-shape head helped him become the most powerful can in the flock. Relatives of the gutsy Captain would tell flock tales of his remarkable keen sense of knowing what time to feed

on the Flats and when to fly to deep water to
raft up during the night. He was rarely ever seen
in broad daylight.

One spring evening, while feeding near
Carpenter's Point, he swam into a lovely young hen
can named Hanna Flats. She was impressed with
his flight abilities. Captain Can could soar at such

unbelievable high altitudes, then dip and dive suddenly into the water. When he performed his stunts and displayed his plumage for her, she would affectionately call him "her cannie." Together they raised a healthy brood of six cans. They were content being a special part of this rick of backs on the Flats.

Captain Can and Hanna, like all good duck parents, guarded their young cans on the Flats and knew from experience the early signs that hunting season was fast approaching. They taught their youngsters that a lantern glowing atop a pushpole at night's end was warning enough that gunners were claiming their blinds or hunting spots along the Flats. Father Can

taught them to listen for sounds of barking retrievers and pointers. Their sharp barks were threatening enough to flush out a flock of railbirds or a group of teal still lingering after a long summer's rest. The good Captain Can and Hanna were still training their six young backs the deadly "game of the game gunners."

On this early morning in November, the prime of duck hunting season, Captain Can and Hanna allowed their children to venture a little further into the Flats. Two of the siblings, Emma Duck and Can Jr., were so busy feasting on the luscious wild celery and

eel grass, they hadn't realized that the strong wind and rough current blew them off course from their family. They found themselves in hunting territory, well within the imaginary line of the Flats, where hunters had been patiently waiting in the waters as early as three fifteen in the morning! Both backs instinctively sensed they were lost. They saw many ricks of ducks: canvasbacks, redheads, blackducks, pintails and even a flock of Canada geese from a distance. Not one canvasback or bullneck looked familiar to them. Their feathers began to shake with fear as they paddled aimlessly through the Flats.

Just beyond them in the bright orange horizon, they saw what looked promising to be an island of backs. "That must be our rick," Can exclaimed hopefully. As they swam closer to the group of cans, with Can Jr. leading the way, they quacked desperately, "Wait for us! Here we are! We're coming!"

The doomed ducks thought they heard their mother's reply, but little did they know, it was the sound of a "duck call" from one of the gunners! Emma and Can Jr. continued to toll behind the stream of ducks.. They had no idea they were falling right into the burlap bags of the hungry hunters. The hunter lay patiently on his back in the sinkbox with his can decoys strategically placed around his sinkbox and through the Flats' waters. The straying ducks were lured directly into the gunner's range!

Suddenly, a shot rang across the water! One impulsive hunter popped out of nowhere, as if he were in the middle of the decoys. As he bobbed in the sinkbox in a crouched position, the double-barrel shotgun fired again! An entire flock of canvasbacks took flight from behind Emma and Can Jr. Fearing for their fowl lives, the two ducks plunged as deep as they could in the gray water. Emma and Young Can were diver ducks, able to swim underwater for as long as fifty

13

yards. They had tolled so closely to the rig, they were afraid to chance the flight. Being young ducks, they had not quite mastered their flight patterns.

Emma and Can swam as fast as their webbed feet could paddle. They resurfaced the water once, exposing only their bills for some air, then dove again. They paddled, resurfaced and dove a second time. Finally, the exhausted ducks sensed that they were in safe territory and waddled up to rest near some stalky, green reeds.

"Goodness, gracious me! You two are certainly lucky ducks!" cried a drake pintail preening himself on the marsh's edge.

It was Professor Pintail, a long time friend and mentor of their father's, Can Sr. Professor Pintail is a highly intelligent drakemaster, originally from the school of thought in Havre de Grace. He is acclaimed to be the utmost authority on duck survival strategies.

The good professor exclaimed in a sharp quack, "Gee, I thought your father would have taught you a few more flight positions and warning signs by now. Your father was at the head of his flock and passed Duck Survival Skills 101 with flying feathers."

Emma shamefully admitted, "It's our fault, Professor, We wandered away from the flock because we were too busy feeding our bills on the thick, wild celery when a strong current blew us off course!"

Now, Professor Pintail, being the well-educated

sprig he was, was quick to understand his naive friends' plight of flight and was not too harsh on the inexperienced cannies. For him, it was a "teachable moment" and he was eager to offer more web-footed wisdom. Professor Pintail was a majestic and slender sprig. He had a prominent brown head and a long, slim white neck that allowed him to streamline with ease across the Flats. His tail was as long and pointed as a fine arrow and his mind was as sharp as a tack.

15

Professor Pintail began his lesson, "Your father must have missed the lesson on sinkboxes that day."

Emma and Can Jr. inquired together, "Sinkboxes?"

"Why, yes, my webbed-footed friends," he exclaimed! The smart sprig lectured, "Sinkboxes are special hunting boats about six feet long and shaped like a human's coffin. The box is surrounded by a wooden deck. Canvas-covered frames or wings are fastened to the deck with hinges. Sinkboxes are usually painted a dull gray so it is difficult for us to see them in the gray water. The sinkboxes are 'camouflaged' in the water. Those gamesters actually set 'dummy ducks' called wingducks on the deck. Some are wooden and

some are iron ducks. The heavy iron ducks are used to sink the box to water level, and the wooden ones are placed on the canvas wings to conceal the hunter. Then they surround the sinkbox with floating ducks, called "decoys," that have an anchor or body weight attached to the bottom to keep them balanced."

Emma spoke in amazement, "Oh, so that's why it's called a sinkbox." She preened her wet breast feathers as she continued to listen to him.

"Exactly!" replied the Professor, extending his wing toward her back. "These clever gunners actu-

ally paint their decoys to look just like us. Some of them are quite artistic, I might add. They stream hundreds of them all around the box to 'toll' us. We are tricked into thinking it is a real flock of ducks and we enter their range of fire."

"Why those waterfowling waterfoolers!" cried Can Jr. "We certainly were lucky ducks."

By this time the noon day sun was shining overhead. Emma and Can Jr. were exhausted from their close "duck call." Emma interjected politely, "Not to interrupt you, sir, but it's getting late in the day. Can you please help us find our way home, back to our rick of cans? We usually rest at Carpenter's Point."

Professor Pintail replied with kindness, "It would be my pleasure. I've been meaning to catch up on some duck talk with your father, anyway."

The three birds began their flight and swim from below Red Point to Carpenter's Point, with the slender, smart sprig at the lead.

Beyond Red Point, Professor Pintail spotted an old acquaintance resting in a small cove of cattails and marsh grass. It was Lucy the Redhead. Lucy was a hen redhead from the family of diving ducks. Although she is called a redhead, she is brownish with a gray wing patch and a blue-gray bill. The drake redheads are known for their bright red plumage.

Lucy gurgled as she slowly turned her head around from a sleeping position and stretched her weak, gray wings. "Well, good morning, Professor Pintail," she groaned.

"Good morning?" he questioned back to her. "It's almost one o'clock in the afternoon," he corrected her.

Lucy squinted her beady eyes and looked up at the bright sun. From its position in the marsh, she could tell he was precise as always.

"So it is," agreed Lucy.

"How are you feeling today, Lucy?" the sprig asked sincerely.

Poor Lucy was recovering from a hunting accident with some gunners in a bushwhack boat. A lead shot slighted her and she had been crippled. She managed to escape when a black lab carried her gently to shore and swam back into the water for a second retrieval.

Lucy moaned, "Oh, my left breast and wing still bother me." She winced, "I have a difficult time taking off in my flight positions and even diving is getting to be painful. I'm no spring duck anymore!"

Professor Pintail sensed Lucy was a little depressed. She had been in seclusion from the other birds, trying to recover from her mishap and staying out of harm's way of the hunters.

Professor Pintail empathized with Lucy, "I'm sorry. I don't have time to visit now. I must get these youngsters back to Captain Can and Hanna. They'll be worrying about them. I promise, on my return I'll stop in and we'll have a chat."

Lucy delighted, "Oh, that would be lovely. I'll plan a special treat for us. Perhaps some eel grass tea and widgeon crisps. I'll look forward to it," she beamed.

The traveling trio waved their wings farewell and continued on their journey to Carpenter's Point.

As they neared Cara Cove and parted the marsh reeds in their swim, they heard a huge flock of Canada geese taking off like the roar of a plane in "V" formation. They were headed to a nearby cornfield to graze on corn as they followed their migratory course southward. It was always a heavenly sight to see them on the Flats.

As they swam and flew across the North East River, they were cautious of gunners. By this time of day, most hunters were done their day of gunning. There were no restrictions on the number of birds shot. Hunters could kill as many as they could carry. It wasn't difficult to shoot them since the thick, wild celery attracted thousands of birds to the Flats. Market hunters would have caught their fill by noon and be on their way to train stations to sell their ducks to fancy restaurants in the large cities, such as Baltimore, Wilmington, Philadelphia and New York. Gunners also sold their birds at the steamboat docks. Market hunters would sell a four pound can for $5.00 to $7.00. This was how they made their living.

From halfway across the Northeast River they could see their flock of cannies. Emma Duck and Can Jr. were elated to be home again. They fluttered their wings in excitement, spraying their duck friends with the cool evening waters.

That evening, Hanna and Captain Can invited Professor Pintail for a delectable dinner. She placed a white tablecloth on a rotted bushwhack boat and created an arrangement with marsh flowers and reeds. Hanna served celery soup, hearts of wild celery, widgeon grass pie and eel grass tea. A meal fit for a special drake friend, Professor Pintail.

After dinner, the two drakes told the six youngsters some of their flock tales and the close "duck calls" they experienced while growing up on the Flats. The six little cans rested in a straight row, wing to wing, on the dry marsh grass: Emma, Can Jr., Candace, Cecil, Cecilia and Baby Hanna.

Captain Can reminisced, "Do you remember the time we flew over to Plum Creek (pronounced crick) in Elkton to attend the wedding of Mayor Mallard's daughter, Mallory, to Millard Duck?"

The Professor recalled, "Oh, how could we ever forget that royal gala. If my memory serves me right, it is Mayor Mallard's ancestors whose portrait is on the Official Seal of Cecil (pronounced Cicil) County."

"That's right," said Can. "They are proud ducks."
Hanna commented, "My, how Mallory made such a
beautiful hen bride!"

Can continued, "I remember distinctly, it
was high tide on the marsh and just
before they exchanged their vows, a
skiffboat with a couple of gunners

drifted past the congregation. One fellow was push-
ing the skiff with a pushpole, while the other aimed
for those little railbirds."

"Phew!" Professor Pintail recollected, "Now that
was a close one!" Good thing they had their minds
and stomachs on railbirds that morning and not on
roast duck dinners!"

After storytelling hour, Hanna told the children that it was time to raft up for the evening. There were Emma and Can Jr., eyes closed with their bills tucked in a sleeping position...snoozing away. Hanna spoke softly, "Just look at those two tuckered darlings!" She was so relieved to have her two cans back with her brood.

Professor Pintail said good night to the rest of Hanna and Can's brood and thanked them for a wonderful evening.

On his return, Professor Pintail visited Lucy Redhead as he promised. She was still a little downhearted, but good ol' Professor Pintail found a way to lift her spirits.

"Lucy," he began, "things could be worse."

"How do you mean?" she wondered.

The sprig counseled, "At least you weren't used as a 'live decoy' like your Great Uncle Robert Redhead. Those hunters put a harness around his neck and attached it to a weighted rig! He was a dead duck in no time."

Lucy reckoned, "Well, I guess you're right. I do have a lot to be thankful for in my life." Then she added, "I guess I'm a lucky duck, too!" They chortled through their bills as they sipped on their eel grass tea.

That night, Professor Pintail flew at high altitude to return to one of his favorite resting spots at Turkey Point. He was as happy as a duck could be on the Flats. He was satisfied to know he had helped his feathered friends survive another day of living and hunting on the Susquehanna Flats.

GLOSSARY

Anchor – a lead weight tied to a decoy to keep it in place

Can – an abbreviation for canvasback; species of diving duck

Back – Another abbreviated word for canvasback

Bullneck – Another name for a canvasback

Bushwhack boat – type of rowboat with one oar for sculling

Decoy – a man-made duck used to lure live ducks close to the hunter

Drake – a male duck. The drake has colorful feathers to attract the hen

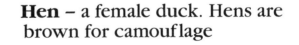

Hen – a female duck. Hens are brown for camouflage

Pintail – species of dabbler duck

Pushpole – an instrument used with a skiffboat to help navigate the boat through the marsh

Raft – a large number of ducks resting on the water

Railbird – a small, hand-sized bird which lives in the marsh

Redhead – species of diving duck

Rick – a large group of waterfowl

Rig – any type of boat used for gunning with decoys

Sinkbox – a coffin-shaped boat with wooden and canvas wings

Skiffboat – a small, slender boat with pointed ends

Sprig – another term for a pintail

Teal – species of dabbler duck which can be found in the summer, both blue-winged and green-winged

Tolling – ducks flying down to decoys in the water

Wingduck – decoy with a flat bottom which is set on the canvas wings of a sinkbox

ABOUT THE AUTHOR: Corinne M. Litzenberg was born and raised in Elkton, Maryland. She received her B.S. in Elementary and Special Education from the University of Delaware and her M.Ed in Curriculum and Instruction from Loyola College in Baltimore. Ms. Litzenberg teaches third grade at Elk Neck Elementary, Cecil County Public Schools. She resides in Elkton with her two children, Todd and Natalie.

ABOUT THE ILLUSTRATOR: David Stehman spent many childhood family vacations in the coastal wetlands of New Jersey, Virginia and Maryland. Elk Neck was always a favorite spot and its natural beauty influenced Dàvid to become a professional artist. Working first as a sculptor and now as an illustrator and graphic designer, David never strays far from the natural world which helped him grow.